C000071199

E.R.A.
A Concise History

J.R.W. Barker

TRANSPORT BOOKMAN PUBLICATIONS

Published in 1992 by Transport Bookman Publications, South Street, Isleworth, Middlesex TW7 7BG.

© Copyright J.R.W. Barker 1992

All rights reserved. Apart from any fair dealing for the purpose of private study, research, criticism or review, or as permitted under the Copyright, Designs and Patents Act, 1988, no part of this publication may be reproduced, stored in a retrieval system, or transmitted in any form or by any means, electronic, electrical, chemical, mechanical, optical, photocopying, recording or otherwise, without prior written permission. All enquiries should be addressed to the publisher.

ISBN 0-85184-049-3

Photoset by Gemini Design
Printed in England by Wizard Printing Services Ltd.

Acknowledgements

The author and publisher are grateful to the Michael Sedgewick Memorial Trust without whose help this book may never have been published.

I should also like to thank the following for their help and encouragement.

Geoffrey Goddard, Michael Gold, Denis Jenkinson, Tony Merrick and his staff, David Sankey of E.R.A. Ltd, Geoffrey Squirrel of Jim Fitzgerald Engineering, Guy Spollon of the E.R.A. Club, Frank Stroud and all his staff at Chaters and Jost Wildbolz.

Special thanks to Peter Hull for dotting the i's and crossing the t's.

I would also like to thank ERA (Engineering Research Applications) for the use of their logo.

Details of the E.R.A. Club can be obtained from Guy Spollon, Arden Grange, Tanworth-in-Arden, Warwickshire.

Dedication

*To my wife Val
and my two boys,
Michael and Jack.*

Contents

Introduction

As the very respected motor racing journalist Denis Jenkinson once said to me: "The trouble with people is they die, but cars don't". What is it about old racing cars, steam trains, aeroplanes, and other vehicles that is so "alive"? They seem to be living beings, having souls.

I find that whenever I stand by a vintage racing car I can feel it wanting to tell me its story – of the characters it has known, the drivers, the mechanics, of the circuits it has raced on and of the races themselves. I feel this never more so than when I am near an E.R A.

Of the seventeen A,B,C and D type E.R A.'s built, sixteen remain, each with a story of its own, and I am sure the ghost of the only one destroyed turns up at race meetings today to watch.

This book is the story of these cars. It covers mainly their history until the outbreak of the Second World War, the period that the cars were designed and built for. Though raced in Grand Prix after the war with some distinction, they were basically make weights, being technically out of date. Some mention is needed to explain the changes that took place to individual cars at this time in their lives. Of the seventeen A,B,C, and D types built, all but one scored at least one victory and the only one which failed to win a race was placed 2nd. Nearly all of these cars are still very active and can be seen competing against each other at hillclimbs, sprints and in vintage race meetings.

E.R.A.'s have raced in nearly every country in the world where racing takes place. They have been raced by many great drivers including Princes, Lords , jazz musicians and drivers from numerous different countries.

E.R.A.'s were very important for British racing. Up until their arrival in 1934 there had not been a British racing car (as distinct from a sports car) able to compete successfully on Continental circuits since the Grand Prix Sunbeams of the early 'twenties'. In the interval, racing in Britain had mainly been between obsolete or near obsolete European G.P. cars, converted sports cars and track specials which could not be raced elsewhere in the world with any hope of success. Brought up via the White Riley on the straights and bends of Shelsley Walsh Hill Climb, the Mountain Circuit at Brooklands and on the natural road circuit taking in the streets of Douglas, Isle of Man, the E.R.A.'s undoubtedly attracted the crowds to the new British road circuits at Donington Park from 1933, the Crystal Palace from 1936 and the Campbell Circuit, part road, part track, at Brooklands from 1937.

E.R.A. history pre-war is one of success and failure but whatever criticism could be levelled at those behind the project it brought Britian firmly back into the international motor racing arena. It is this which helped build the success achieved post-war by the likes of B.R.M., H.W.M., Connaught, and Vanwall in later years by Lotus, Cooper, Brabham, Tyrrell, and March and up to date with McLaren and Williams who dominate motor racing worldwide.

I have kept the seasons 1934-39 section brief as far better descriptions of those years have already been written (see Bibliography). My main purpose is to tell the story of A,B,C and D type E.R.A.'s. I include other E.R.A. projects, bringing the story up to date with the E.R.A. Mini. There are two short biographies of the drivers, Prince Birabongse Bhanutej Bhanubanbh 'B.Bira' and Raymond Mays because of their importance and impact on E.R.A. history.

With each chassis there are listed their pre-war drivers together with their pre-war placings i.e. wins, 2nd and 3rd placing plus heat wins and fastest time of the day for hillclimbs and sprints.

E.R.A. stood for English Racing Automobiles and after changing hands in the 1950's became known as Engineering Research Applications. This company is still involved in specialized research and consultancy to the automotive industry worldwide.

I believe the E.R.A. story to be about great personalities; cars and humans alike. I do hope you enjoy it.

J.R.W. Barker,
Walton-on-Thames
April 1992

CHAPTER ONE

How it all started

In 1932 Raymond Mays, probably the first motor racing sponsorship hunter, and his close friend Peter Berthon, attracted help from the Riley Motor Company in the building of a special hillclimb car based on a 12/6 Riley production car with a 1,500cc engine.

Murray Jamieson, already recognized in the sport for his work on engines and especially superchargers, became an engineer on the project. With Berthon and Jamieson looking after the engineering of the car and the talented Mays the driving, the car, which became known as the "White Riley", was built in time for the 1933 racing season. It was successful in sprint races and hillclimbs for which the car had been specifically built and at which Raymond Mays had been so successful in his racing career. Mays was approached by Humphrey Cook to take the project into a new era.

Raymond Mays in the 1½ litre supercharged 6 cylinder "White Riley" at Shelsley Walsh in 1933.

R1 unpainted at Bourne 1934, later to become R1A. Note the F. Gordon Crosby badge.

Cook was a very wealthy amateur racing driver and very patriotic to boot. He could see the potential of a 1,500cc "Voiturette" racing car in the Riley and supplied the finance for Mays to form a company to build and race cars both in England and abroad. He planned to take on the then dominant French and Italian manufacturers, Bugatti, (nearing the end of his influence on Voiturette racing) and Maserati.

The very talented designer, Reid Railton, of the Brooklands racing track firm Thomson and Taylors was commissioned to design and build the first chassis in the winter of 1933. He was later responsible for Sir Malcom Campbell's and John Cobb's land speed record cars among others. The engine was to be based closely on the 6 cylinder Riley engine already modified by Jamieson and Berthon.

Work was now underway to build a team of factory cars with production models available for sale to customers. Prices for these cars in 1935 were £1,700 for the 1,500c.c. version and £1,500 for the 1,100c.c. version. The company and the cars were to be called E.R.A.: English Racing Automobiles.

These lovely racing cars were built and assembled at the E.R.A works at Bourne, Lincs.

CHAPTER TWO

The Seasons 1934-1939

When the first E.R.A. appeared in 1934 it broke no new ground, with a conventional chassis on the lines of an earlier Maserati. It was likened to a roller-skate with its driver perched high in the cockpit. Any detractors must have been silenced by the time initial handling problems had been sorted. The car became a legend for its phenomenal acceleration.

Following impressive first outings in 1934 orders for customer cars arrived to be raced alongside those of the works team.

1935 was a season in which the E.R.A.'s confirmed their potential. They won almost every major "Voiturette" race in Europe that they entered. This was what they had been built for. Experiments with Zoller supercharger to give more power resulted in less reliability.

1936 was to be the year of Richard Seaman and his Delage and Count Carlo Felice Trossi with his Maserati. When they did not win, "B.Bira" and R2B "Romulus" did. E.R.A.'s raced on with reliability problems from the new engine/supercharger modifications though an improved "B" type chassis did make things better.

1937 brought still further improvements to chassis, brakes and suspension giving increased life against tough Maserati competition. With Seaman and his Delage having moved on, E.R.A. wins came from Arthur Dobson, Raymond Mays, "B.Bira" and Eugen Bjornstad in Europe.

By 1938 even for the one-off "D" type, results began to get thin. Up until now always dominant on the home front, E.R.A.'s were no longer the force they had been in 1936. With an E.R.A. Europe was the place to race for fun. No longer was a race win guaranteed. The Alfa Romeos Tipo 158 arrived and it was to be these cars that were to dominate up to the war and in post-war Grand Prix racing. This was the case until the end of 1951 when these cars were ruled out by formula change. Also available to the private entrant was the Maserati 4CL model which proved superior to the dated E.R.A.

The 1939 season was shortened for British teams with the imminent hostilities putting paid to any serious assault on Europe. An added complication was the works concentration on the new E-Type.

Raymond Mays C.B.E.

CHAPTER THREE

Raymond Mays C.B.E.
1899-1980

Raymond Mays was born into a family with interests in the woollen industry. The family firm was in Bourne, Lincolnshire where Mays was brought up. Mays saw action in the 1914-18 war serving as an officer in the Grenadier Guards.

Upon his return from war he went to Cambridge. He started his long racing career in 1921 racing a Speed Model Hillman nicknamed "Quick Silver". Mays emerged from Cambridge the typical English gentleman that the 1920's seemed to produce. He built his career from hillclimb and Brooklands race successes in various makes of car including the above Hillman, through two Bugattis (Cordon Rouge and Cordon Bleu) A.C., T.T. Vauxhall Villers, Mercedes, Invictas and of course the "White Riley" which started the E.R.A. project.

Mays was always charming and persuasive with a gift for securing support, both financial and technical, throughout his own career and post-war for the B.R.M. (British Racing Motors) project.

Always elegant in his tailored silk racing overalls, Mays disguised his not inconsiderable talent. He was always very quick on the shorter events such as hillclimbs and sprints and he often as not held lap records even if he didn't win the longer races. At one time he held the Crystal Palace and Brooklands' Campbell and Mountain Circuits lap records all at once.

Mays was a legend at the famous Shelsley Walsh Hillclimb, winning many events from his first appearance in 1923 to his last in 1950. His record driving E.R.A.'s was astounding: 20 race and heat wins plus 12 F.T.D.'s and class wins in hillclimb and sprints were achieved on R1A, R2A, R3A, R4B/C/D and R12B/C.

Mays dedicated his life and family home to motor racing. Eastgate House, Bourne, Lincolnshire was the operation headquarters for both E.R.A. and B.R.M. (post-war). In 1978 Raymond Mays received the C.B.E. for his services to British Motor Racing. He died in Stamford Hospital, Lincolnshire not far from Bourne in 1980.

CHAPTER FOUR

Prince Birabongse Bhanubandh – "B.Bira" 1914-1985

Prince Bira was born into the Royal Family of Siam (now Thailand) on the 15th. July 1914, grandson of King Mongkut, the main character from "The King and I".

At the age of thirteen in 1927 he was sent to England to complete his education. In 1929 the young prince went to Eton. He was to become an all round athlete. After leaving Eton Bira took sculpture lessons from Charles Wheeler, A.R.A. This was a great love of his, leading to his work being exhibited at the Royal Academy in London.

Prince Bira lived with his guardian and first cousin once removed, Prince Chula Chakrabongse, who was six years his senior. Prince Chula was to become Prince Bira's sponsor, mentor and team manager during his racing career, deriving much pleasure himself from the team management, race strategy and pit organisation.

It was Prince Chula's money that bought and ran the cars Prince Bira was to race, starting in 1935 with a Riley then an M.G. K3 Magnette. The events undertaken in these cars were to give no indication of the successes which were to follow with E.R.A.'s R2B, R5B and R12B/C together with the ex-Whitney Straight Maserati. The Princes knew that to progress in the sport a more powerful car which could be raced in "Voiturette" races in Europe would have to be purchased. What could be better than a new E.R.A.?

On Prince Bira's twenty-first birthday Prince Chula presented him with R2B, a 1,500cc supercharged E.R.A. It was to be painted, as all their cars, in "Bira" blue and run by their own "White Mouse" team.

Prince Bira won many races in the three E.R.A.'s that he raced, descriptions of which are in the relevant R2B "Romulus", R5B "Remus" and R12B "Hanuman" sections of this book. Prince Bira quickly became a "natural" being smooth, fast, consistent and sympathetic mechanically with his mounts. A mistake or a crash was very rare and his driving was very fair, making him safe to dice with at close quarters.

Prince Bira won the much coveted B.R.D.C. (British Racing Drivers Club) Road Racing Gold Star in 1936, '37 and '38. This award made him the equivalent of the British Racing Champion. His talent also brought him drives in cars away from the "White Mouse" stable.

Following the war Prince Chula soon stopped his patronage of Prince Bira's racing due to ill health and disillusionment with post-war racing. Without his cousin's support "B.Bira" soldiered on against the works teams in Grand Prix racing and retired in 1955 after winning the New Zealand Grand Prix driving another classic racing car, the Maserati 250F.

During his career Prince Bira raced the following makes of racing car; Riley,

M.G., E.R.A., Austin, Delage, Delahaye, Alfa Romeo, Maserati, B.M.W., Simca-Gordini, H.R.G., Ferrari, Osca and Aston Martin. He was never to drive for a great Grand Prix team pre or post-war. His undoubted talents deserved better than this. His racial background would not have fitted into the pre-war Nazi Germany sponsored Mercedes-Benz or Auto-Union teams.

Bira was at home in the air, being a glider pilot instructor during the war and was also a very keen yacht racer which is the sport he turned to on his retirement from Motor Racing. He was also a powered aircraft pilot and after the war wrote a book called "Blue Wings Over Bangkok" about his flight from England to Thailand in his twin engined Miles Gemini with his wife – and dog. Later he ran a Thai airline.

Prince Bira was a remarkably talented man and a great racing driver. He died in London in 1985.

Footnote: The "Bira Blue" referred to in the text is a mid blue which was discovered by Prince Chula on a young Dutch girl's dress. The prince liked the colour so much that he obtained a small piece from the dress from which he matched the shade.

Prince Bira

CHAPTER FIVE

R1A

Built 1934
Driven by: 1934-39   Places: 1st.-6, 2nd.-4, 3rd.-4

Raymond Mays   Prince zu Leiningen
Humphrey Cook   Mrs Kay Petre
Richard Seaman   Hon. Brian Lewis
Tim Rose-Richards   Eugen Bjornstadt
Oliver Bertram

R1A started life painted light green and following various changes of colour scheme is now light green again. R1A was the prototype and first built E.R.A. works car. Completed in May 1934 and fitted with a 1,500cc supercharged engine, R1A was fitted with an E.R.A. "Rising Sun" badge designed by the famous motoring artist, F. Gordon Crosby, the only car to be so adorned. This soon disappeared for the three rings badge we know today designed by Squadron Leader "Pingo" Lester, a friend of Raymond Mays.

R1A's initial appearances in the hands of Raymond Mays were fraught with problems, as is the case with many new cars, though the car's potential could be seen. Modifications were made which soon ironed out the car's handling problems mainly caused by the steering drop arm having been mounted in the wrong place, and from there it never looked back.

Towards the end of the 1934 season race wins and hillclimb class wins were being achieved by R1A and Mays.

Raymond Mays in R1A at Shelsley Walsh 29th September 1934 where they achieved a class win. Above the right rear wheel stands Whitney Straight.

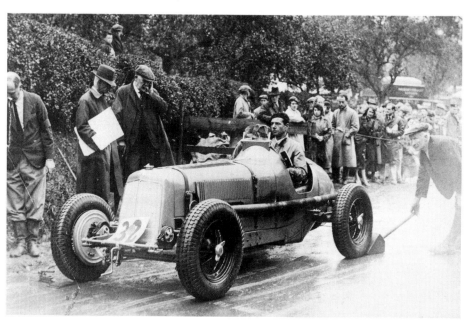

This pair also took Standing Start one mile (96.08mph) and one kilometre (85.35mph) world records as did Humphrey Cook with R2A (see R2A).

For the 1935 season Raymond Mays was using R3A and then R4B, and R1A was used more by Cook and as a works car for its various invited drivers. Humphrey Cook used R1A in low key handicap and speed events with success against relatively poor opposition. And why not indeed, as the financial benefactor of the project. Whilst the new works entered driver, Richard Seaman, awaited the completion of his R1B, he and R1A raced at Donington and achieved 2nd. place behind C.E.C. "Charlie" Martin on a 2.3 litre Bugatti.

The second half of 1935 brought a 3rd. for Tim Rose-Richards and R1A on the difficult Nurburgring. This was E.R.A.'s first major success against the European opposition with four E.R.A.'s in the first five places: Mays(R3A) 1st., Seaman(R1B) 4th., and Cook(R2A) 5th.

During the 1936 season R1A raced only twice. Once was in the hands of the glamorous darling of the press, Mrs Kay Petre, who retired in her race. Kay was the only woman to race an E.R.A. pre-war. R1A was then shipped to the U.S.A. for the Vanderbilt Cup and driven by Hon. Brian Lewis to 15th. in a race won by the great Tazio Nuvolari driving a 4.1 litre V12 cylinder 12C-36 Alfa Romeo.

The E.R.A. works team sold R1A at the end of 1936 to the Norwegian ice racing specialist Eugen Bjornstadt. In his first race with an E.R.A. Bjornstadt's sideways style brought R1A its first international race win at the very tight and twisty Turin circuit beating more modern Maseratis and E.R.A.'s. The Norwegian's rubber smoking style also achieved further success, two 3rds. and a 7th.

R1A was by now four years old and rather thrashed by hard driving. Though

6th July 1935
British Empire Trophy.
Oliver Bertram R1A
followed by Pat Fairfield
R4A. The Brooklands
banking is seen clearly in
the background.

9

sold in 1938 to W.E. Humphries, R1A was not seen again until after the war.

In 1947 R1A was raced to victory twice by Reg Parnell, through whose hands many E.R.A.'s passed.

These wins were achieved in Sweden on ice circuits. R1A was modified in the late 40's as most E.R.A.'s were in an attempt to stay competitive.

One of the major modifications to R1A was a lowered bonnet profile to give better streamlining.

R1A was completely rebuilt to as near as original by Tony Merrick (see A.J.M.1) during the late 70's early 80's. The current owner is Jost Wildbolz, a Swiss driver, who races R1A fitted with a 1,500cc. s/c engine, regularly in Historic races.

CHAPTER SIX

R2A

Built 1934
Driven by: 1934-39   Places: 1st.-1, 2nd.-3, 3rd.-2
Humphrey Cook
Tim Rose-Richards
Raymond Mays
Nicky Embiricos
A.C. Pollock

R2A started life painted works light green and following changes in colour scheme is now dark green. R2A was the second car built for E.R.A.'s financial benefactor, Humphrey Cook, who was the typical English Gentleman; Public School, Oxford educated, and very wealthy, which allowed him to indulge in his passion for motor racing.

Cook first started racing at Brooklands before the Kaiser war of 1914-18. He was happy at the start to fund an all British contender to take on the foreign opposition. He raced R2A mainly in 1934 and 1935. R2A won its first race, a handicap event at Brooklands, though later on the same day Cook spun the car round and up an earth bank, very nearly turning it over.

R2A spent most of its early life with a 1,100cc supercharged motor fitted so that Cook could race in this lower engined capacity class. As was very fashionable in the 1920's and 1930's Cook and Mays, R2A and R1A respectively, undertook to break the Standing Start World Records at Brooklands for the mile and the kilometre. This was a brave undertaking as Brooklands was notoriously bumpy but both managed the feat. R2A achieved 88.91mph on the mile and 79.75mph on the kilometre.

Cook raced R2A until September 1935 and then retired from racing except for racing R12C briefly in 1937.

R2A, being a works' car, was fitted with a 1,500cc s/c engine and used by Mays as well as Cook in the European races but without much success. By the end of 1935 the works had had their use out of R2A and sold it off to Nicky Embiricos for the 1936 season.

Embiricos was a Greek who had previously raced a Bugatti Type 55 at Brooklands with some success. Embiricos painted R2A grey and undertook a 1936 season racing at the larger events in Europe with a best result being a 3rd. in Monaco behind R2B (Bira) and the fated R3B (Lehoux).

For the 1937 season Embiricos employed the famous mechanic/engineer Giulio Ramponi who had worked wonders on Richard Seaman's Delage and R1B as well as Whitney Straight's Maseratis. He modified the front suspension of R2A to a "state of the art" Tecnauto independent suspension system and also lowered the car's suspension and radiator height without aesthetically changing the shape too much. This system is in fact still fitted to R2A.

6th July 1935
British Empire Trophy,
Brooklands.
Humphrey Cook in R2A.

1947
George Abecassis in R2A
with a modern shaped
radiator and Tecnauto
front suspension.

Unfortunately Embiricos crashed R2A at its first meeting in modified form and did more damage to the car than himself but he decided to retire. R2A then passed into the hands of A.C. Pollock who raced it up to the outbreak of the war but without many decent results.

Immediately post-war R2A was given further bodywork alterations by George Abecassis, one of the partners in H.W.M. (Hersham and Walton Motors). Like R1A, R2A was also used in ice circuit racing in Sweden. This car too was owned by Reg Parnell though he never drove it. It also spent some time in the Far East.

R2A won the very first V.S.C.C. Richard Seaman Trophy Race driven by George Harwell at Silverstone in 1950.

The car has been returned to its 1937 specification and is owned and raced on a regular basis by Brian Classic with a 1,500cc s/c engine fitted.

CHAPTER SEVEN

R3A

Built 1934
Driven by: 1934-39   Places: 1st.-5, 2nd.-7, 3rd.-0
Raymond Mays   Tom Wisdom
Tim Rose-Richards   Charlie Martin
E. Von Delius   Roy Hesketh
Norman Black

R3A started life in the works light green. Following on from R1A, fitted with a 1,500cc s/c engine and R2A, fitted with a 1,100cc s/c engine, R3A was fitted with a 2 litre s/c engine. As a works' car R3A was used almost exclusively by Raymond Mays until sold at the end of 1935. R3A was used in 2 litre form for record breaking attempts, hillclimbs and non-"Voiturette" (1,500cc formula) events.

R3A's 1934 season comprised three events. It was driven on public roads to its first event, a hillclimb at Shelsley Walsh, which it and Mays, the hillclimb "Maestro" won. R3A was 2nd. in its first race at the Brooklands Autumn meeting to the 2.9 litre Maserati of Whitney Straight. This race also gained the pair the Mountain Circuit Class E lap record. This was followed up with a successful attempt on the World's Standing Start kilometre which Mays and R3A took at 89.73mph. This followed on from R1A 1,500cc and R2A 1,100cc records earlier that year. As this was the outright record, R3A's other achievement was to become the smallest capacity car ever to hold such a world speed record.

The 1935 season was marked by the lack of reliability for the works entered cars. Mays did again win the Shelsley Walsh hillclimb with R3A and with a 1,500cc engine fitted won the "Voiturette" event at the infamous Nurburgring in Germany. This was E.R.A.'s first such win in Europe. What is more, Mays had never before seen this daunting 14 mile twisting circuit and had to learn the course in his Bentley Saloon the week before the event.

Both Tim Rose-Richards and E. Von Delius drove R3A for the works but without success.

With a 1,500cc engine fitted, R3A was sold to Norman Black for the 1936 season. He shared the car with Tom Wisdom. This pair produced nothing from R3A and Charlie Martin bought the car for the 1937 season.

Martin and R3A won their first event together on the Avus banked circuit as a supporting event to the German Grand Prix. R3A and Martin achieved a staggering lap in practice of 123.1mph, nearly 200kph, and won the event at an average 119.63mph in front of 380,000 spectators. This pair went on to achieve many 2nd. places throughout Europe for the rest of 1937.

R3A spent 1938 up for sale and eventually was purchased by Roy Hesketh, a South African, who raced only twice in his native country before the war. Post-war R3A stayed on in South Africa and was raced by Basil Beall with some success. The car returned to England following Beall's death in 1957 from an

*6th May 1935
J.C.C. International
Trophy at Brooklands.
Raymond Mays in R3A*

*31st May 1935
Mannin Moar, Isle of Man.
Raymond Mays in R3A.*

accident unrelated to the sport. R3A was in a most original condition having missed the modifications and developments of the late 1940's and 50's that other E.R.A.'s incurred in England. R3A was sold in 1988, fitted with a special 1,900cc s/c engine.

The car has been rebuilt by Tony Merrick (see AJM1) for its present owner, Mr Takahashi, a japanese collector. It has reappeared painted works light green after many years painted red and is now fitted with a 2 litre engine and blower.

CHAPTER EIGHT

R4A

Built 1935
Driven by: 1935-39
Pat Fairfield
Norman Wilson

Places: 1st.-7, 2nd.-6, 3rd.-6

R4A started life painted white but is now raced in blue. R4A was the first E.R.A. to be sold to a customer. It was bought by Pat "Skidder" Fairfield, a South African who was born in England. Whilst over here at University, like so many young men from wealthy families, he took up motor racing. He started with Freddie Dixon's Rileys then bought R4A which he had run by the works for 1935.

R4A was fitted, like R2A, with a 1,100cc supercharged version of the standard 1,500cc s/c E.R.A. engine. This was to enable R4A to take advantage of the 1,100cc class and handicap against the larger capacity cars. Fairfield and R4A won their third race when they won the Mannin Beg, a 200 mile race on the Isle of Man, for cars up to 1½ litres, beating his mentor Freddie Dixon (Riley) and others with larger engines.

29th May 1935. Pat Fairfield in R4A winning the Mannin Beg in Douglas, Isle of Man.

R4A and Fairfield suffered during 1935, as did R1B and Richard Seaman, with poor preparation by the works. Nevertheless, a couple of wins on alternate weekends at Donington Park (Nuffield Trophy) and Dieppe (Voiturettes Grand Prix) were significant. The latter event was especially important as R4A was still fitted with a 1,100cc s/c engine against the larger capacity opposition. 1935 was rounded off with a handicap win at Brooklands.

Fairfield, like Seaman, was disenchanted with the works but went it alone into the 1936 season with R4A, unlike Seaman who sold R1B. 1936 started with a visit to South Africa and a third place behind a couple of much larger engined Bugattis. On its return to England R4A was fitted with a 1,500cc s/c engine. R4A and Fairfield were rewarded with their best result for the year of 2nd. to Seaman on a 2,600cc Maserati at the British Empire Trophy at Donington Park.

Disappointment at Monaco followed with a disqualification due to a push start for R4A after Fairfield had spun to avoid others' mistakes on the second lap.

During May 1936 Fairfield rejoined the works for the balance of the season. Seven races and two changes of colour scheme for R4A (works green followed by black) brought four retirements. Things had not changed. The highlight of the season was a second at the Picardy Grand Prix in France in both heat and final.

For 1937 Fairfield stayed with Bourne as a works driver using R4A in some early season races in South Africa achieving three wins from four starts. R4A and Fairfield's last race together, fittingly at Donington Park where their careers

1948
Bob Gerard's R4A with sloped radiator which it retains to this day.

together started, achieved a 3rd. As a works driver, Fairfield then drove works cars R4B and R12C. Unfortunately Fairfield was killed at Le Mans that year driving a 328 Frazer Nash-B.M.W.

R4A was sold to fellow South African Norman Wilson with a 1,100cc s/c engine fitted once more. He raced R4A both at home and abroad until the war, in which he was killed whilst serving in the South African Air Force.

The 1938 and 1939 seasons brought much activity for R4A but without the successes nor the retirements experienced at Fairfield's hands. After all, an A type was getting old and with a 1,100cc s/c engine, uncompetitive.

During the war the car passed into the hands of Reg Parnell before the late Bob Gerard purchased it. R4A was then given the same modernised sloped radiator as R6B.

Bob Gerard and his wife Joan mainly hillclimbed R4A with much success. It was to be one of three E.R.A.'s they owned, the others being R6B and R14B.

R4A still races today fitted with a 2 litre s/c engine, owned and driven by Sir John Venables Llewelyn.

CHAPTER NINE

R1B

Built 1935
Driven by: 1935-39   Places: 1st.-4, 2nd.-3, 3rd.-6
Richard Seaman
G.F. Manby Colgrave
"Buddy" Featherstonhaugh
W.E. "Billy" Cotton
Wilkie Wilkinson
Arthur Dobson

R1B started life painted black and is now raced in that same colour. Of all the E.R.A.'s built R1B is the only car which helped build the meteoric rise in one driver's career. That driver was Richard Seaman, who quickly rose through the ranks to become a member of the great pre-war Mercedes-Benz Grand Prix team.

Seaman's association with E.R.A.'s must have been a love-hate one. Following the promising 1934 start for E.R.A.'s, Seaman talked his wealthy mother into buying him an E.R.A. Raymond Mays, always quick to spot talent and a promotional opportunity for E.R.A., offered Seaman the chance to run as a team member.

This arrangement didn't work out very well. The E.R.A. works preparation was not terribly good and Seaman became disenchanted and took R1B away from the factory at Bourne. Preparation of R1B was entrusted to the great mechanic, Giulio Ramponi, and results finally started to happen. From August 4th. to September 29th. in 1935 Richard Seaman and R1B dominated the Voiturette racing scene in Europe. They gained wins in the Coppa Acerbo at Pescara, Italy, Prix de Berne in Switzerland, Masaryk Grand Prix at Brno in Czechoslovakia and also achieved a 1st. in class and 2nd. overall in the internationally important hillclimb at Freiberg in Germany.

After a disappointing season in Richard Seamans's eyes, he sold R1B and stunned the racing world by buying a 1927 Grand Prix 1,500cc supercharged Delage for the 1936 season! With this Delage heavily modified by Ramponi, Seaman really rubbed the noses of E.R.A. in it by taking the 1936 season by storm. By 1937 he was a Mercedes Grand Prix driver.

R1B passed into the hands of G.F. Manby-Colgrave, an amateur driver, who raced it on only a handful of occasions. He sometimes shared the driving with Jazz musician "Buddy" Featherstonhaugh.

For 1937 and until the outbreak of war, Billy Cotton the famous band leader and later television personality owned and raced R1B. Racing mainly at Brooklands, Cotton achieved a couple of wins in handicap races. He did share the driving at some events with his mechanic Wilkie Wilkinson. Wilkinson and Arthur Dobson also substituted for Cotton when his professional engagements clashed.

R1B is another E.R.A. which has raced uninterrupted to the present day still

20th July 1935
Dieppe, France.
No 10 Richard Seaman R1B,
No 4 Raymond Mays R1A,
No 12 Pat Fairfield R4A,
No 20 Howe in the Delage
that Seaman raced in 1936.
Behind seaman is "B. Bira"
in R2B.

1947, Jersey
No 16 Wilkie Wilkinson R1B,
No 15 H.L. Brooke R7B.

fitted with a 1,500cc s/c engine. It is also in a remarkably original condition. This is due to the work of the late Patrick Marsh who did so much for the vintage racing scene. The car is entered today by Patrick's widow for Duncan Ricketts to race, and is quite capable of beating other E.R.A.'s with 2 litre engines.

27th August 1938
J.C.C. 200 mile Race at
Brooklands on the
Campbell Circuit.
No 14 Billy Cotton R1B,
No 16 Reggie Tongue R11B
and eventual winner No 18
Johnny Wakefield R14B.

CHAPTER 10

R2B "Romulus"

Built 1935
Driven by: 1935-39   Places: 1st.-16, 2nd.-10, 3rd.-13
Prince Birabongse Bhanubandh "B.Bira"

R2B was supplied with the customer standard 1,500cc supercharged engine fitted and was painted "Bira" blue from new and did not take on the yellow chassis and wheels until 1939 when Thailand was given its national racing colours.

R2B was not christened "Romulus" until 1936 when R5B "Remus" joined the "White Mouse" team. Both cars sitting side by side looked like twins hence the names.

R2B was the second E.R.A. customer car, purchased by Prince Chula as a 21st. birthday present for his cousin Prince Bira on 15th. July 1935.

R2B, untested, was shipped from Bira's birthday party to its first race meeting at Dieppe in France. Though nobody other than Bira raced R2B, Raymond Mays did run in R2B before Bira's first taste of his new mount. R2B and Bira took 2nd. place to Pat Fairfield and R4A(1,100cc s/c) after Mays (R1A) and Seaman (R1B) retired due to mechanical problems as they often did during that season.

Another 2nd. place from a front row grid position was Bira's and R2B's next best result at the 1935 Berne Grand Prix in Switzerland to the now almost unbeatable Seaman and R1B. Other results that season were on the British mainland and all were in the top five. A Fastest Time of the Day came at a speed trial, the only such event that Bira was allowed to undertake, Prince Chula not being interested in hillclimbs or sprints. The other achievement for the 1935 season was no retirements, unlike the other E.R.A.'s.

R2B, now named "Romulus" and Bira's 1936 season couldn't have started better. A win at Monaco against tough opposition came after the young prince had a nasty incident at Donington the week before. He was driving R5B "Remus" when a stone shattered his goggles leaving splinters of glass in his eye.

The pair's next win was a classic dice between themselves and R4B and Raymond Mays at Brooklands. The finish was very close with the lead changing twice on the last lap, the result going R2B and Bira's way. There was only one second between them at the finish.

A 2nd. in the Isle of Man to the all conquering Richard Seaman and his Delage was another good result. A 3rd. place at the German Nurburgring behind the Maseratis of Count Trossi and Tenni was E.R.A.'s best result in this difficult race. Bira and "Romulus" followed this with their 3rd. and last win of the season at the Picardy Grand Prix in France. This was achieved against all the top opposition in Europe and after a particularly close dice with Fairfield and R4A.

R2B had an excellent year especially as the Delage of Seaman swept almost all before it and events won were achieved against tough opposition.

In 1937 Bira and R2B "Romulus" had a hard year racing extensively in Britain and Europe. R2B was now dated, though still reliable, but with Maserati concentrating on their 6CM Maserati Voiturettes, results in Europe were thin on the ground. Results at home were excellent and the pair were almost unbeatable. They also started their battles with Arthur Dobson and R7B which continued almost until the war.

By 1938 R12C had replaced R2B "Romulus" which was by now uncompetitive in Europe and was raced by Bira only on the mainland of Britain. In eleven races R2B "Romulus" won no less than six times. The car's reliability was second to none with failure to finish only occurring once due to a puncture in a match race at Crystal Palace with Dobson and R7B.

In 1939 Bira was still racing the obsolete R2B "Romulus", even relying on the car for a 3rd. at their last race before the war at Albi, France, due to Bira's accident with R12C the previous week. Bira himself was still recovering at this event.

17th July Crystal Palace, London Grand Prix.
"B. Bira" in R2B "Romulus" won two heats and the final.
Note the "White Mouse" on the mirror.

Bira and R2B "Romulus" had a very special relationship and a successful career with many fine races both at home and abroad and some very close finishes.

"Romulus" was raced a few times post-war and now, still owned by Prince Chula's daughter, is to be seen now and then at very special events. A truly special car, and in very original condition having benefited from a rebuild by Bill Morris who owns R12B & R12C.

1st July 1939 Crystal Palace. "B. Bira" in R2B "Romulus".

CHAPTER ELEVEN

R3B

Built 1936
Driven by:
Marcel Lehoux

Places: 1st.-0, 2nd.-2, 3rd.-0

R3B was a works car and always raced in light green. Of the seventeen A, B,C, and D type E.R.A.'s built R3B is the only car not to have survived.

It was built as a works car in 1936 for Marcel Lehoux. Lehoux was a French Algerian who joined the works team for the 1936 season at the age of 48. He brought with him a vast amount of experience which he had gained in Grand Prix and Voiturette racing mainly in Maseratis, Alfa Romeos and Bugattis which of course had been the formula's mainstay until E.R.A.'s arrived on the scene.

Sadly R3B's career was short but nonetheless relatively successful. It raced only outside the British mainland, with its most notable achievement being 2nd. at Monaco to Bira on R2B "Romulus". It raced at some famous circuits; Monaco, Isle of Man, Nurburgring, Picardy, Albi and Deauville.

Up to its last race R3B had been fitted with a 1,500cc s/c engine, however, at its last race at Deauville it was entered for a Formula Libre race and had a 2 litre engine with a Zoller supercharger fitted. Whilst lying in 3rd. position R3B was hit from behind by the hard charging Farina on an Alfa Romeo who was leading the race and lapping Lehoux. The impact caused R3B to roll twice and catch fire. Poor Lehoux died later from injuries sustained and R3B was deemed too badly damaged to be rebuilt. Salvagable parts of R3B, however, were used up on other cars and kept as spares.

R3B, therefore, lives on in a small way in others, though rumours of the existence of the chassis R3B could one day lead to a reconstruction completing the set of the seventeen E.R.A.'s. If this ever happens the authenticity of the chassis will be rightly questioned, having been missing from the scene for so long.

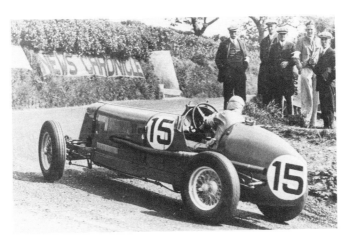

28th May 1936
Douglas, Isle of Man.
Marcel Lehoux in R3B.

CHAPTER TWELVE

R4B/C/D

Built 1935
Driven by: 1935-39
Raymond Mays
E. Von Delius
Pat Fairfield
Arthur Dobson

Places: 1st.-26, 2nd.-8, 3rd.-1

2nd May 1936
J.C.C. International
Trophy.
2nd place for Raymond
Mays in R4B. Note paint
work damage due to spilt
methanol fuel.

R4B started life painted the "works" E.R.A. light green and changed to the black in 1936 along with all the other works cars. R4B was numerically the most successful, the most developed, through changes to B,C, and D types though maybe not having the charisma of R2B "Romulus".

R4B was to spend almost all of its life driven by Raymond Mays with special modifications to suit him. In all its guises R4B spent much of its competition time on the short sprints either hillclimbing or at speed events, capitalizing on May's talent in these events and also using the E.R.A.'s phenomenal acceleration. R4B/C/D mostly used a 2 litre s/c engine but also used the 1,500cc s/c and 1,100cc s/c version of this motor when necessary.

R4B started racing in the 1935 season and a reference to its first race is a must

although the car was shared at the German Grand Prix at the Nurburgring by Mays and the German, Von Delius (who had crashed R3A in practice) and they retired. It was at this race that the great Tazio Nuvolari in an Alfa Romeo beat the might of the German Mercedes-Benz and Auto Union on home ground much against the odds.

The balance of that season was spent winning events such as hillclimbs at Shelsley Walsh, an event Mays had made his own over the years, particularly with R4B/C/D.

1937 brought R4B up to "C" type specification. This entailed modifications which are detailed in the technical section at the end of this book. R4B was modified from "B" type to "C" type changing the steering geometry to suit Mays. As a child Mays had sustained an injury to his left arm and R4C was modified with the bell crank on the left side, opposite to the other "C" types, and also had an angled steering wheel to help compensate for May's reach.

In May's hands R4C was amazingly fast though as most "works" cars, prone to retirement due to either poor preparation or to overworked mechanics. As R4C was a development car for new ideas, particularly engine and supercharger modification, it was not surprising that problems arose. If R4C and Mays finished a race they usually won. Wins and F.T.D.s came at Donington, Crystal Palace, Picardy G.P, Brooklands, Phoenix Park and Shelsley Walsh.

1938 was to bring R4C up to "D" type specification after an unsuccessful trip to South Africa. For its "D" type modifications the largest change was a new chassis which was drilled for strength and lightness.

2nd August 1937 J.C.C. International Trophy. 1st place for Raymond Mays in R4C.

27

*7th August 1939
Raymond Mays in R4D.
1st in the Campbell Trophy
at the last race meeting
ever held at Brooklands.*

*Post-war Ken Wharton
hillclimbing R4D.
Twin rear wheels are for
better traction.*

The 1938 season was similar to 1937 with a second win at the Picardy Grand Prix in France and two F.T.D.s at Shelsley Walsh. From sixteen races and hillclimbs R4D and Mays achieved 8 wins or F.T.D.s. Again the balance were mostly retirements.

For 1939 Arthur Dobson raced R4D twice with one win at Brooklands before a disenchanted Mays bought R4D and raced independently of the works. Wins or retirements followed and Mays and R4D found their way up to the top of Shelsley Walsh again, their sixth F.T.D. and 7th. class win.

R4D and Mays competed together until 1950 and no prizes for guessing where they achieved results. The cars had a very active and successful 1950's in the hands of Reg Parnell, Ron Flockhart and Ken Wharton.

R4D looks much as it did pre-war but has undergone almost uninterrupted development since it started life as R4B. Very little of the car can be said to be 1930's with much replaced due to fatigue, wear and tear of the constant competition. R4D is one of the fastest cars on the vintage scene beating many a younger Grand Prix car. It is fitted with a 2 litre Zoller blown engine and is owned by Anthony Mayman who races it with consistent success, holds the hill record for pre-war cars at both Shelsley Walsh and Prescott and is a triple winner of the V.S.C.C.'s premier race for pre-war Historic Racing Cars, the Richard Seaman Trophy race, 1989-91. Mays won the R.A.C. Hill Climb Championship with R4D in 1947 and 1948, as did Ken Wharton in 1954 driving R4D and a Cooper-JAP.

CHAPTER THIRTEEN

R5B "Remus"

Built 1936
Driven by:1936-39
Prince Birabongse Bhanubandh "B.Bira"
Tony Rolt
St. John Horsfall

Places: 1st.-8, 2nd.-6, 3rd.-5

R5B is painted light blue with yellow wheels unlike R2B and R12B/C which are light blue with yellow wheels but also have yellow chassis. The reason for this is that Thailand was given its country's racing colours of yellow chassis and light blue body in 1939 by the International Sporting Body after R5B had been sold.

R5B was the second E.R.A. owned by Prince Chula for his cousin "B.Bira" to race. Bira named this one "Remus" and R2B "Romulus" after the twins from Roman mythology. Of the three E.R.A.'s raced by Bira "Remus" was the least successful and therefore sold on to Tony Rolt after a short career with the "White Mouse" equipe.

Bira only raced "Remus" during 1936 with success both at home and abroad but not up to the standards set by "Romulus" or the subsequent R12B/C "Hanuman". 1936, it must be remembered, was the year that Richard Seaman and his Delage swept all before them wreaking revenge from his appalling year with the E.R.A. works team in 1935. "Remus" won the Albi Grand Prix although neither Seaman nor the works Maserati team were present.

"Remus" spent 1937 being used for spares by the "White Mouse" equipe until built up and sold to Tony Rolt in 1938. Rolt used R5B during 1938 and was very active both at home and abroad with most success being at home in handicap type events.

In 1939, the last season before the outbreak of the war, R5B had its best victory by winning the British Empire Trophy at Donington in Rolt's hands. Modifications were made by Freddie Dixon, the Riley specialist tuner and racing driver. Rolt then went into partnership with St. John Horsfall who drove R5B for what remained of the season. R5B spent most of the year racing at Brooklands and Horsfall achieved something no other driver ever had in an E.R.A. He raced on the very bumpy outer circuit and twice finished 3rd. at the speeds of 124.51mph and 124.82mph, a very brave effort indeed on what was a car that certainly wasn't designed for this type of track.

"Remus" was raced during 1947/8 and 9 by that motor racing character John Bolster, famous for his "Bloody Mary" specials. "Remus" did not escape modifications to both engine, by way of twin superchargers, and suspension, in the form of hydraulic shock absorbers. The car is now thankfully back to its pre-war state, apart from a subtle lowering of the radiator line.

It was with Bolster driving that the pair had a big accident in which "Remus" was rolled and Bolster hurt quite badly.

*29th May 1939.
St John Horsfall in R5B
"Remus" finishes 3rd on
the Brooklands outer
circuit in the Locke King
Trophy Race.*

1948 Zandvoort.
John Bolster in R5B
"Remus".
Note lowered bonnet
height.

It has raced since the war, without major interruption, to be one of the most successful E.R.A.'s on the V.S.C.C. scene. R5B was fitted from new with a 1,500cc s/c engine but has raced with a 2 litre engine for some years now. "Remus" races on in "Bira" blue only. Today the car is owned and raced by Ludovic Lindsay whose late father Patrick also raced "Remus" with much success in Vintage and Historic events, winning the Richard Seaman trophy race at Oulton Park seven times between 1961 and 1981, after Bill Moss had won with 'Remus' in 1957 and 1958.

R1A 1990

R2A 1989

R3A 1991

R4A 1989

R1B 1988

R2B 1987

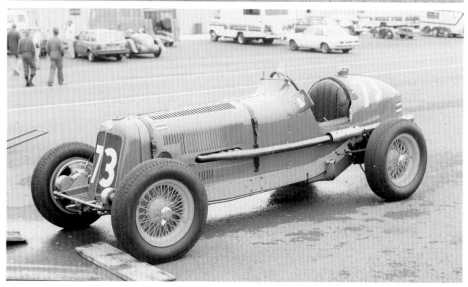

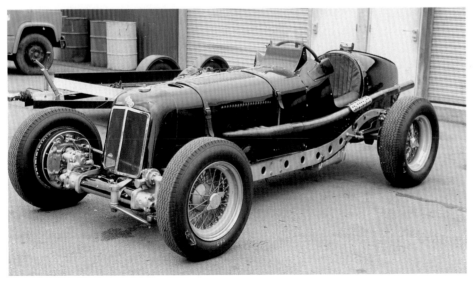

R5B 1991

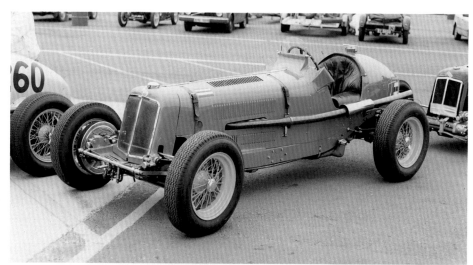

**R6B 1986
before rebuild**

R6B 1991

R7B 1989

R8B/C 1991

R9B 1991

R10B 1991

R11B 1991

R12B 1988

R12C 1988

R14B 1991

AJM1 1991

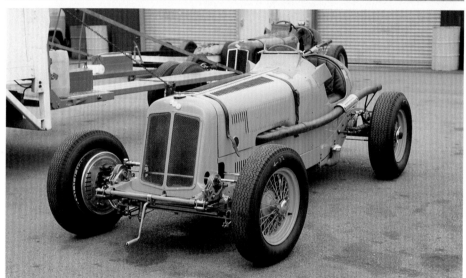

GP2 1990

CHAPTER FOURTEEN

R6B

Built 1936
Driven by: 1936-39   Places: 1st.-5, 2nd.-5, 3rd.-4

Dr. J.D.Benjafield   Johnnie Wakefield
Earl Howe   Kenneth Evans
William Everitt   Peter Monkhouse
D.L. Briault   Robin Hanson
Kenneth Evans   Reg Parnell
Ian Connell

R6B started life painted green and following various paint jobs is now dark blue. The car was fitted as it is now with a 1,500cc supercharged engine.

R6B was driven by more people before the war than any other E.R.A., more even than the works R1A and R3A. The reason for this large number (11) was mainly due to R6B being used in races in which a co-driver was required and it also changed hands a number of times.

The first owner of R6B was "Bentley Boy", Dr. J.D.Benjafield, winner of the 1927 Le Mans with Sammy Davis in a Bentley. Benjafield raced R6B twice only before selling it to Douglas Briault who had previously raced an M.G. and Alta at Brooklands. R6B was raced to the end of 1936 with a best placing of 3rd. at the J.C.C. 200 mile race at Donington partnered by Kenneth Evans of the racing family of Denis and Doreen Evans. Briault then sold R6B on to Ian Connell, yet another experienced Brooklands racer.

The first thing Connell did with R6B was to ship it over to Sweden for some ice racing on frozen lakes. This was achieved by the fitting of spiked tyres to give grip. Connell was relatively successful against the locals though all the races were won by E.Bjornstadt who later owned R1A. Ian Connell thereafter only raced and hillclimbed in Britain and Ireland until he sold the car, having used R6B throughout 1937 and 1938. He also experimented with twin superchargers but without success.

In 1939 R6B was purchased by Mrs. Hall-Smith for Robin Hanson to drive who had previously raced her M.G. and Maserati. Hanson won two races before war broke out, one each at Brooklands and Donington. R6B was given one last outing before the hostilities by Reg Parnell but with a 1,100cc s/c engine fitted.

Bob Gerard purchased R6B after the war and, like R4A, it was given a streamlined sloped radiator. Its history in Gerard's hands is uncertain as it appears to have been used as a source of spares for R4A and R14B. It was raced very consistently between 1958 and 1967 by Sid Day, who won the Richard Seaman Trophy in it in 1960 and 1967, and after some inactivity, it was sold fairly recently to a large auction house, which specialises in this type of car, and has since been raced by one of their executives, Jeffrey Pattinson. The car now has new bodywork which looks not unlike that of R5B Remus.

May 28th 1936
Douglas, Isle of Man.
W. Everitt in R6B.

CHAPTER FIFTEEN

R7B

Built 1936
Driven by: 1936-39   Places: 1st.-6, 2nd.-18, 3rd.-6
Arthur Dobson
Cyril Paul
Charles Brackenbury

R7B started life with a 1,500cc supercharged engine and was painted white with a very distinctive chromium plated radiator cowl. Although Arthur Dobson bought R7B, Cyril Paul raced it for its first three races with a best placing being 3rd. on the Isle of Man. The bespectacled Dobson had gained experience at Brooklands with various cars which included a Bugatti and a Riley. He came from a racing family.

R7B was owned and raced by Dobson to the outbreak of war. He raced almost exclusively on the British mainland, Isle of Man and Ireland with one trip to the Modena G.P. Italy in 1938, placing 3rd. Dobson, as well as owning R7B, also raced for the works and Billy Cotton from time to time driving R1B, R4D and R12C. Dobson raced for approximately half of 1936 with R7B having entered Cyril Paul in some races.

1937 brought more activity for the pair and their 1st race win in a Brooklands handicap. 1937 also brought the 1st race with a close 1st./2nd. finish between "B.Bira" and Dobson, the first of many, especially at the tight twisty Crystal Palace Circuit in London. The duels between these two young men started to capture the imagination of the public and the, what we could call today "tabloid press". Numerous Bira v. Dobson stories appeared during the late thirties, though away from the circuits these two were friends and had been river boat cruising together with their wives.

Charles Brackenbury raced R7B once in 1937 at Donington when Dobson was winning with R12C in the J.C.C. 200 mile race. Dobson's 1937 wins in the works R12C showed his true talent (see R12B). He matured as a driver after this experience to make 1938 R7B's most successful season.

Most of the "B.Bira" R2B "Romulus" versus A.Dobson R7B races were won by the former, but these races were extremely close.

Each driver had complete trust in the other in their wheel to wheel dicing. A match race took place between the two at Crystal Palace but, unfortunately, like most of these types of events, it was a failure. Bira's R2A "Romulus" got a puncture making it a non event.

Another of Dobson's and R7B's achievements was being the first E.R.A. home in 6th. place in the Donington Grand Prix behind the German "Titans" of Tazio Nuvolari Auto Union – 1st., Hermann Lang Mercedes-Benz – 2nd., Richard Seaman Mercedes-Benz – 3rd., H.P. Muller Auto Union – 4th. and M. von Brauchitsch Mercedes-Benz – 5th. Although six laps down it was indeed an

*28th May 1936
R.A.C. Light Car Race,
Isle of Man.
No 11 Cyril Paul R7B 3rd
chased by No 17 "B. Bira"
R2B "Romulus" 2nd.*

*22nd October 1938
Donington Grand Prix.
Arthur Dobson in R7B.
The metal side panels
widen the bodywork to
comply with Grand Prix
regulations.*

achievement of merit against such dominant opposition.

In 1939 Dobson concentrated on the new E.R.A. G.P.I. which must have been frustrating (see G.P.I.) and raced R4D. Therefore he only raced R7B seven times including heats with six races at Crystal Palace with a 2nd. to none other than "B.Bira" and R2B "Romulus" for the last time.

It was raced in 1946, 47 & 48 by Leslie Brooke throughout Europe and with some success. This car retained its identity. Purchased in 1960 by Dudley Gahagan, who still races R7B today, it is painted red, and is practically in its original condition but is fitted with a 2 litre s/c engine. A car with real charisma.

22nd October 1938 Donington Grand Prix. Herman Muller Auto Union passes Arthur Dobson in R7B. They finished 4th and 6th respectively.

CHAPTER SIXTEEN

R8B/C

Built 1936-39
Driven by: Places: 1st.-1, 2nd.-5, 3rd.-3
Earl Howe
Piero Taruffi

R8B/C was purchased by Earl Howe in 1936 with the standard 1,500cc supercharged engine fitted. It was run in his own colours of blue body with silver chassis and wheels. Earl Howe started racing at 44 years of age, an age when most drivers think of retiring. Howe raced in many different makes both at home and abroad, including winning Le Mans with Sir Henry Birkin in an Alfa Romeo. He was very influential in racing circles, being President of the B.R.D.C. (British Racing Drivers Club).

Howe decided to run his E.R.A. R8B for the 1936 season and was to have his car looked after by the works at Bourne. As with Seaman before with R1B, the preparation and therefore reliability left much to be desired with poor places and retirements to show for the season.

For the 1937 season Earl Howe's own mechanics took charge of the car's preparation. Following two 2nds. and one 3rd. in races in South Africa early in the year, R8B returned to Britain. Earl Howe and R8B had a very serious accident at Brooklands in May of that year. Howe made a mistake whilst leading "B.Bira" in his 2.9 litre Maserati. In the accident R8B was rolled and Howe thrown clear. Injuries to both were serious but happily both were racing together again later in 1937. A highlight on their return was taking part in the Donington Grand Prix against the might of Auto Union and Mercedes who soundly beat the home opposition. R8B and Earl Howe had the honour of being the first E.R.A., albeit three laps down, in 7th. position.

Howe and R8B spent the winter of 1937/38 in South Africa with a win in Cape Town in January 1938 before returning home. Whilst in South Africa R8B was driven by the great Italian, Piero Taruffi, to a 2nd. place.

R8B was totally rebuilt to "C" type specification in 1938. This rebuild took in parts from other cars in particular R4B/C's, though the car then became R8B/C which Howe used through 1938 and what was left of 1939 before the war.

For the 1938 season Howe did rejoin the works team with a best result of 2nd. in heat at the Picardy Grand Prix in Peronne, France. In Earl Howe's hands R8B/C was raced on three continents; America, Africa and Europe.

After the war R8B/C was another car to pass through the hands of Reg Parnell who sold it to Cuth Harrison who kept the car until 1951. During this time R8B/C underwent very many changes to chassis and more importantly to the bodywork. During 1948/49 Harrison completely transformed R8B/C as no E.R.A. had been before. He rebuilt the car with a "D" type chassis, new brakes and a very smart contemporary bodywork. The car was raced in this form by many drivers, the best

*2nd October 1937
Donington Grand Prix.
Earl Howe in R8B
finished 7th.*

*1950 Silverstone.
Cuth Harrison in R8B/C
with highly revised
bodywork.*

of whom were Harrison, Brian Shawe-Taylor (who crashed the car heavily) and Graham Whitehead. Good results were achieved throughout its pre-V.S.C.C. days.

In the late 1970's and early 1980's R8B/C was totally rebuilt by its present owner, Bruce Spollon, to its 1938 specification, and is now one of the most beautiful E.R.A.'s racing in its blue and silver paint job. R8B/C is fitted with a 2 litre s/c engine.

CHAPTER SEVENTEEN

R9B

Built 1936-39
Driven by:
Dennis Scribbans   R.E.Ansell
Charlie Martin   Charles Brackenbury
Hector.G.Dobbs   Brian Shawe-Taylor

Places: 1st.-8, 2nd.-3, 3rd.-6

R9B was originally painted cream but is now painted white with dark red wheels. A 1,500cc supercharged engine was fitted as it is today. R9B was purchased by Dennis Scribbans, a stockbroker from Birmingham. Scribbans had never raced cars before the purchase of R9B but he had hillclimbed some years before at Shelsley Walsh. Bearing these facts in mind their 1936 season's results on paper look astonishingly good. From the twelve events he and R9B undertook they achieved two 1sts, one 2nd, four 3rds., a Fastest Time of the Day, three retirements and was once unplaced. They also achieved a lap record in F class at Brooklands on the Mountain Circuit.

Looked at in perspective, however, these results were from handicap events against relatively poor opposition with wins on days when most E.R.A.'s were racing abroad for international glory. R9B and Scribbans did win their first race together, something only achieved by themselves and R2A/H.Cook, though R3A, R4D and R12B did win their first events. This was some achievement over the rest, the car and driver being so virginal to the sport.

Also in 1936, Scribbans loaned R9B to Charlie Martin and was rewarded with a win at Donington against greater opposition in the Nuffield Trophy.

1937 by comparison was a disaster for R9B and Scribbans with nothing of note achieved.

R9B, having never been outside of the British mainland, was sold to R.E.Ansell who was also from Birmingham. Ansell raced and hillclimbed R9B through 1938 and 1939 without any significant achievements. Wins in handicap events and F.T.D.'s in small hillclimbs obviously brought pleasure to R9B's driver who enjoyed his amateur pastime.

Their last outing together before the war was R9B's only overseas event, at Berne in Switzerland (The Swiss Grand Prix). They finished 6th. in the Prix De Berne voiturette race and 13th. in the Grand Prix itself with such greats as Lang, Caracciola and Von Brauchitsch on Mercedes-Benz, Muller and Nuvolari on Auto Unions. That was on 20th. August 1939. Germany invaded Poland on the 1st. September – World War II had commenced.

Post-war R9B was raced and hillclimbed a great deal by R.E.Ansell and his cousin G.E.Ansell. It was during this time that R9B had two big accidents, one at a hillclimb in Jersey driven by George Bainbridge and the second a spectacular roll while driven by Geoffrey Ansell. This was during the 1948 British Grand Prix and was captured by Movietone News.

The car then passed into the hands of its former mechanic, Brian Shawe-Taylor, who raced it until he retired following a big accident in R8B/C.

The car is owned and raced still by Peter Mann, having been a Richard Seaman Trophy winner in 1966 driven by Peter Waller and in 1978 driven by Peter's brother, Chris Mann.

*4th July 1936
Donington Park.
Charlie Martin in R9B
winning the Nuffield
Trophy.*

CHAPTER EIGHTEEN

R10B

Built 1936-39
Driven by: Places: 1st.-3, 2nd.-4, 3rd.-9
Peter N. Whitehead
Peter D. Walker

Purchased in 1936 by Peter Whitehead, R10B was painted black, the colour it still is today. R10B was raced by Whitehead and his friend Peter Walker with whom he had also shared his Alta in 1935. This pair raced the car exclusively before the war and also raced it afterwards for a time.

During the 1936 season R10B was raced by the two Peters in the United Kingdom and Ireland with their best result being F.T.D. at a hillclimb in Yorkshire, driven by Whitehead. A 2nd. in the Nuffield Trophy at Donington and a 3rd. in the Donington Grand Prix when both Whitehead and Walker shared the driving in R10B must have been the highlights of the season. The young drivers faced more experienced opposition there than at some of the handicap events

26th September 1936.
Phoenix Park, Dublin.
Peter Whitehead in R10B.

that they had placed well at during that year.

In 1937 Whitehead did venture abroad to France and Italy with R10B but without success. Whitehead drove R10B more often than Walker and they also co-drove in the Isle of Man. There they achieved 5th. place in the rain behind the following E.R.A.'s: 1st. R2B Bira, 2nd. R4C Mays, 3rd. R12C Fairfield, 4th. R11B Tongue.

For the 1938 season Whitehead took R10B to Australia and won the Australian Grand Prix, an event held on a loose surface track. Whilst in Australia Whitehead also achieved F.T.D. at a hillclimb before returning to Brooklands for one last race in 1938.

1939 found Whitehead and R10B in South Africa for the winter though the visit was disappointing with two retirements. Whitehead and R10B finished their pre-war career with 2 3rds. and a 2nd. and Peter Walker scored a 9th. and 7th. in heats at Crystal Palace, his first drive in R10B for nearly two years.

Whitehead and Walker continued to race R10B after the war. Both these young men learnt much from driving R10B, Walker gaining a reputation for spectacular cornering. These two drivers went on to win Le Mans in 1951 for Jaguar and between them drove Ferrari, B.R.M., Maserati and Alta racing cars post-war. R10B races today fitted with a 1,500cc. supercharged engine as it did pre-war.

R10B was an early Richard Seaman Trophy race winner when it was held at Silverstone, the driver being Jack Williamson in 1954.

It has been totally rebuilt to 1930's specification and is owned and raced by Nick Mason when his commitments with the rock group "Pink Floyd" allow.

CHAPTER NINETEEN

R11B

Built 1936-39
Driven by:
Reggie Tongue
Hon. Peter Aitken

Places: 1st.-6, 2nd.-4, 3rd.-9

R11B started out painted dark green with a 1,500cc s/c engine fitted. It now runs in silver with a 2 litre s/c engine and is affectionately known as "Humphrey", the name Reggie Tongue christened it, after Humphrey Cook.

R11B was purchased in 1936 by Reggie Tongue. He was an experienced amateur driver having raced at Brooklands with an Aston Martin as well as with the same K3 M.G. Magnette that started Whitney Straight's and Richard Seaman's careers. With R11B Tongue undertook racing both in the U.K./Ireland and abroad, racing extensively during 1936. He was a competent and steady driver with race positions coming from sympathetic driving.

The short bursts of speed required for hillclimbs were to be the area of much success for R11B and Tongue in 1936 with wins in such events in Geneva in Switzerland, Freiburg in Germany and Shelsley Walsh in England. The biggest win for Tongue and R11B came in the Irish Cork 200 mile race against "B.Bira" and "Remus" R5B following R5B's retirement. Representing Oxford, a win came the pair's way at the last meeting of the year at Brooklands in the Oxford and Cambridge race. 1936 was R11B's most successful pre-war year.

1937 had Tongue and R11B travelling mainly around Europe taking part in "Voiturette" races. Though no wins were recorded they did finish well in some mid-season races in Italy and France with bests 2nd. and 4th. in heats. This gave an aggregate 3rd. in the Albi Grand Prix in France behind the E.R.A.'s of Mays (R12C – a works car before passing into Bira's hands) and Charlie Martin (R3A).

After 1937 Tongue sold R11B on to Hon. Peter Aitken who never raced R11B abroad. Tongue replaced the obsolete E.R.A. with a "State of the Art" Maserati 4CL "Voiturette". Aitken had raced various cars before R11B including Maserati, Delage and Alfa Romeo mainly at Brooklands.

Aitken took R11B to South Africa for the winter season 1938-39 races placing 2nd. at Cape Town. During 1939 on their return R11B and Aitken raced only at Brooklands, Crystal Palace and Donington with some wins and good places mainly in handicap events. Aitken also spent time on his own Alfa-Aitken project, which simply put was half an Alfa Romeo "Bi-motore".

Post-war R11B passed from Reg Parnell to Peter Bell for John Bolster to drive. The car was given a crash gearbox replacing the pre-selector one plus a 2 litre engine that Parnell had built up using Riley parts. Later the car was given the Murray twin supercharger engine that Bolster had used in "Remus" and in which he had crashed. Sadly in this form St. John Horsfall was killed at the Daily Express Trophy meeting at Silverstone in 1948. R11B rolled twice, a similar fate to that which had befallen Bolster and "Remus", but this time poor Horsfall was not thrown clear.

Later in Ken Wharton's hands R11B was very successful in hillclimbs and sprints in lightened form with the engine moved back 3 inches to improve road holding, a 10 gallon sprint fuel tank fitted and lighter radiator, the dry sump 5 gallon oil tank removed and the engine converted to wet sump. He won the 1953 Hill Climb Championship driving R11B and a Cooper-JAP.

It is still a fast car raced by its current owner Martin H. Morris who won the Richard Seaman Trophy race eleven times with it between 1961 and 1986 after the car had also won the race in 1959 driven by Douglas Hull.

16th May 1936.
Cork, Ireland.
Reggie Tongue in R11B
winning the Cork 200 Mile
Race.

CHAPTER TWENTY

R12B "Hanuman" II

Built 1936-39
Driven by: Places: 1st.-16, 2nd.-1, 3rd.-2
Raymond Mays
Pat Fairfield
Humphrey Cook
Arthur Dobson
Prince Birabongse Bhanubandh "B.Bira"

R12B is painted in the same colour scheme as R2B, light blue body, yellow chassis and wheels, the national racing colours of Thailand.

R12B has had an interesting life with modifications and total rebuilds which have spawned R12C (see R12C). R12B was the last works car built and started life with a 2,000cc. s/c motor and was painted the new works colour of black. This followed a change from the previously used light green which may have come about following the fatal accident of Marcel Lehoux and R3B (see R3B).

R12B was built late in the appalling 1936 season for the works. Raymond Mays, nevertheless, achieved F.T.D. at a Shelsley Walsh hillclimb and a win at Brooklands, though it must be noted with a 2 litre motor.

For 1937 R12B underwent the rebuild bringing it up to "C" type specification with the Porsche type designed independent front suspension, lockhead hydraulic brakes, new zoller supercharger and a 1,500cc. s/c engine. Pat Fairfield (see R4A) had become a full works driver and used R12C as well as R4C and his own R4A until his untimely death in June of that year at Le Mans. Fairfield and R12C won two events, one at Crystal Palace and the other just a week before his death at Donington in the Nuffield Trophy. R12C had a larger fuel tank than standard and, unlike the others, was able to go through the race on one tank with no need to refuel. After the sadness of Fairfield's death R12C went on to win four of the next six events in which it competed during the rest of 1937, the other races ending in retirements. These race wins were as follows: Albi G.P., France: 3rd. in heat one with Humphrey Cook drafted in to replace Fairfield, 1st in heat two with Raymond Mays driving bringing an aggregate win. (It should also be noted that Cook had his last race in R12C). Berne G.P., Switzerland: 1st. driven by the new English star, Arthur Dobson (see R7B), 1st. J.C.C. 200 mile race, again Dobson, and 1st. Siam Trophy at Brooklands driven by Mays.

The works sold R12C to Prince Chula, cousin of "B.Bira". It was their third E.R.A. for their "White Mouse" stable. Chula often purchased cars which had been successful in the previous season and R12C certainly was that. Chula, in keeping with the tradition of naming their E.R.A.'s i.e. R2B "Romulus", R5B "Remus", named R12C "Hanuman".

In 1938 "B.Bira" raced R12C with wins coming at Brooklands (twice), Donington and Cork, Ireland with the retirements coming at the all important international

3rd July 1937.
Isle of Man.
Pat Fairfield in R12C
lifts right front wheel on
their way to 3rd place.

10th June 1939.
Donington Park.
"B. Bira" in R12C
"Hanuman" wins the
Nuffield Trophy.
The car is painted blue
body with yellow chassis
and wheels.

"Voiturette" events at Picardy, France and Berne, Switzerland.

"B.Bira" raced R12C only once in 1939 and won the Nuffield Trophy at Donington, achieving his 4th. win of the season from four starts, the other events being won in R2B and his Maserati 8CM. Then came a big shunt seriously damaging R12C at Rheims in France in practice. Bira escaped with minor cuts and bruises.

A "B" type chassis and suspension were used in the rebuild, a "C" type chassis being unavailable due to the imminent outbreak of war. The salvageable parts from R12C were used plus new spares. Once rebuilt this car reverted to R12B and was named "Hanuman II".

It is thought that the chassis used in the rebuild could have been that of the original R8B Howe chassis, see R8B/C.

Post-war R12B won its first event in "B.Bira's" hands before being sold. It competed on a regular basis until sold to Rhodesia, which is where the current owner, W.R.G. "Bill" Morris, bought it. Bill Morris still owns R12B and is responsible for its and other E.R.A. rebuilds.

The car won the Richard Seaman Trophy race in 1968 driven by David Kergon.

CHAPTER TWENTY ONE

R12C "Hanuman"

Rebuilt 1980 (see R12B "Hanuman II")

R12C was rebuilt through the sixties and seventies to be completed in the eighties. By rights it should not be mentioned in this book as it has no pre 1940 history. This reconstruction, however, used new and used E.R.A. parts giving us a "C" type E.R.A. racing car as near as possible to R12C as raced by "B.Bira" and owned by Prince Chula in the thirties prior to the accident at Rheims in practice for the Coupe de la Commission Sportive. The chassis is the original one (see R12B) which was deemed too badly damaged in 1939 to be repaired. R12C is named "Hanuman" as was the original R12C. It races regularly today and is painted like R12B and R2B, light blue body, yellow chassis and wheels.

The person responsible for the rebuild is the current owner, Bill Morris, who also owns R12B. He enters the car on a regular basis for A.K. "Tony" Stephens.

CHAPTER TWENTY TWO

R14B

Built 1938-39
Driven by: Places: 1st.-2, 2nd.-2, 3rd.-6
Johnny Wakefield

R14B raced in pale blue by Wakefield but is now painted dark green. It was the last "B" type E.R.A. fitted with a 1,500cc s/c engine, built and sold to a private competitor, Johnnie Wakefield in 1938. Wakefield started racing motor cars in 1936 and raced an Alta and a Maserati before buying R14B.

By 1938/39 the E.R.A.'s were becoming obsolete against more modern Alfa Romeos and Maseratis. Wakefield, however, raced R14B, which was fitted with a "C" type Zoller supercharged engine to good effect in the U.K. at the road racing type circuits at Brooklands, Donington Park and Crystal Palace. R14B in fact ventured from these shores only twice, the most memorable being to Berne in Switzerland where Wakefield finished 3rd. in both heat and final. R14B and Wakefield's main achievement here was being the first E.R.A. across the line in the final behind the two Maseratis of Hug and Bianco.

One weekend later came R14B's greatest success at the 200 mile Junior Car

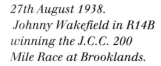

27th August 1938.
Johnny Wakefield in R14B
winning the J.C.C. 200
Mile Race at Brooklands.

Club race at Brooklands. Wakefield showed maturity and skill beating the best the British racing scene could offer; Bira's 2.9 litre Maserati, Chris Staniland's 2.9 litre Multi-Union, Evans 2.9 litre Alfa Romeo and numerous E.R.A.'s with drivers including Mays, Dobson and Earl Howe. Following this R14B's other outing abroad brought retirement at Phoenix Park, Ireland.

Later in 1938 R14B was to win and finish second in two handicap races for which the Brooklands Circuit was famous. The last decent result for this partnership was in October 1938 when they finished 3rd. at Brooklands in the Siam Trophy race when Prince Bira on R12C and Arthur Dobson on R7B fought one of their famous duels which R12C won.

Having no luck with R14B in the early races in the 1939 season Wakefield felt R14B to be no longer competitive and he bought the very latest 4CL Maserati with which to race. He went on to be very successful, winning important races at Naples, Peronne and Albi becoming one of the sport's fast rising stars.

Wakefield unfortunately was killed in the Fleet Air Arm during the war but R14B's story does not end there.

Bob Gerard bought this car post-war making it his third.

Gerard modified R14B as he had R4A and R6B, lowering the bonnet line which is still evident today.

Gerard did give the car a smooth streamlined radiator cowl giving it a very

1947 British Empire Trophy, Isle of Man. Bob Gerard in R14B.

distinctive shape. The car won many races post-war particularly in Ireland, Jersey and the Isle of Man, and was 3rd in the British G.P. at Silverstone in 1948 and 2nd in 1949 behind the latest 4CLT Maseratis.

The car today retains a 1930's style radiator, though lowered, together with a 2.2 litre s/c engine. The owner, Donald Day, still races the car from time to time, having owned the car since 1958.

R14B won the 1956 Richard Seaman Trophy race driven by J.T. Stuart.

1948 Silverstone, British Grand Prix. Bob Gerard in R14B finishes 3rd with new revised bodywork.

CHAPTER TWENTY THREE

A.J.M.1

Rather as R12C's reconstruction should not appear in this book neither should A.J.M.1's! But again, here is a car built in the 1980's from 80% original E.R.A. parts by a well respected vintage racing preparation specialist.

Anthony J. Merrick (hence the chassis no.) used to prepare and race R1A but when it was sold by its owner he decided to turn his pile of spare parts into a 'B' type E.R.A. Tempted by R3B's chassis number Merrick took the honest route and with the approval of the V.S.C.C. and other E.R.A. owners made A.J.M.1.

A.J.M.1. is raced regularly in the original light green works colour and has a 1,500cc s/c engine fitted.

It is usually driven by Chris Mayman, cousin of Anthony Mayman, who owns the car along with R4D.

CHAPTER TWENTY FOUR

Technical Specifications

CHASSIS

Frame:	A and B type channel section, C type box section
Front suspension:	A and B type semi-elliptic and Hartford friction shock absorbers C type Porsche trailing arms with transverse torsion bars and Girling Luvax hydraulic shock absorbers
Brakes:	A and B type Girling mechanical, C type Lockheed hydraulic
Wheels:	Rudge Whitworth
Tyres:	A and B type Front 16x5.25 Dunlops Rear 16x6.50 Dunlops Front 18x5.25 Dunlops Rear 16x6.50 Dunlops

DIMENSIONS

Wheelbase:	96ins. (2438mm.)
Front track:	52.5ins. (1333mm.)
Rear track:	48ins. (1219mm.)
Height:	44ins.(1118mm.)
Dry Weight:	18cwt.

ENGINE

No. of cylinders:	6 in line
Capacity:	1,100cc (1,088cc) Bore 57.5mm Stroke 69.8mm 1,500cc (1.488cc) Bore 57.5mm Stroke 95.2mm 2,000cc (1.980cc) Bore 62.8mm Stroke 107mm
Valves:	2 per cylinder inclined overhead with 2 high set camshafts and short pushrods
Cylinder Head:	Aluminium
Cylinder Block/ Crankcase:	Cast iron with 3 main bearings
Crankshaft:	Manufactured from forged steel billet supported on 3 main bearings
Carburation:	Single side-draught S.U. carburettors
Ignition:	Single plug per cylinder Lucas Magneto
Supercharger:	A and B types Roots/Jamieson, C type Zoller
Brake Horse Power	A and B type 150h.p. at 6.500r.p.m., C type 240h.p. at 7.500r.p.m.

TRANSMISSION

Clutch:	None
Gearbox:	Armstrong-Siddeley Wilson 4 speed pre-selector
Final drive:	Prop-shaft enclosed in torque tube to bevel drive rear axle

CHAPTER TWENTY FIVE

Results 1934-1939

The following list gives results where A,B,C & D type E.R.A.'s finished in the first three placings at major events during 1934-1939. It does not include heats, hillclimbs, sprints or small national races/handicaps.

Date	Race	Driver	Car	Result
1934				
6th October	Nuffield Trophy, Donington Park	Mays	R1A	1st
1935				
29th May	Mannin Beg, Douglas, I.O.M.	Fairfield	R4A	1st
16th June	Eifelrennen, Nurburgring, Germany	Mays	R3A	1st
		Rose-Richards	R1A	3rd
13th July	Nuffield Trophy, Donington Park	Fairfield	R4A	1st
20th July	G.P. De Dieppe, France	Fairfield	R4A	1st
		Bira	R2B	2nd
15th August	Coppa Acerbo, Pescara, Italy	Seaman	R1B	1st
25th August	Prix De Berne, Bremgarten, Switzerland	Seaman	R1B	1st
		Bira	R2B	2nd
29th September	Masaryk G.P., Brno, Czechoslovakia	Seaman	R1B	1st
1936				
11th April	Coupe Prince Rainier Monaco	Bira	R2B	1st
		Lehoux	R3B	2nd
		Embiricos	R2A	3rd
16th May	Cork 200 mile Car Race, Ireland	Tongue	R11B	1st
28th May	RAC International, Light Car Race Douglas, I.O.M.	Bira	R2B	2nd
		Paul	R7B	3rd
14th June	Eifelrennen, Nurburgring, Germany	Bira	R2B	3rd
21st June	G.P. De Picardy, Peronne, France	Bira	R2B	1st
		Fairfield	R4A	2nd
		Howe	R8B/C	3rd
4th July	Nuffield Trophy, Donington Park	Martin	R9B	1st
		Dobson	R7B	2nd
		Whitehead/Walker	R10B	3rd
12th July	G.P. d'Albigeois, Albi, France	Bira	R5B	1st
26th July	Coppa Ciano, Livorno, Italy	Embiricos	R2A	2nd
23rd August	Prix De Berne, Bremgarten, Switzerland	Embiricos	R2A	2nd
		Tongue	R11B	3rd
29th August	J.C.C. 200 Mile Race, Donington Park	Howe	R8B/C	2nd
		Briault/Evans	R6B	3rd

Results

Date	Race	Driver	Car	Result
1937				
18th April	Circuit of Turin, Valentino Park, Italy	Bjornstadt	R1A	1st
		Tongue	R11B	3rd
24th April	Coronation Trophy, Crystal Palace	Fairfield	R12C	1st
		Dobson	R7B	2nd
25th April	Coppa Principessa, Di Piemonte, Naples, Italy	Bira	R2B	2nd
		Bjornstadt	R1A	3rd
30th May	Avusrennen, Avus, Berlin, Germany	Martin	R3A	1st
3rd June	RAC International, Light Car Race Douglas I.O.M.	Bira	R2B	1st
		Mays	R4C	2nd
		Fairfield	R12C	3rd
12th June	Nuffield Trophy, Donington Park	Fairfield	R12C	1st
		Dobson	R7B	2nd
		Mays	R4C	3rd
27th June	G.P. De Picardy, Peronne, France	Mays	R4D	1st
11th July	G.P. d'Albigeois, Albi, France	Mays/Cook	R12C	1st
		Martin	R3A	2nd
		Tongue	R11B	3rd
22nd August	Prix De Berne, Bremgarten, Switzerland	Dobson	R12C	1st
		Mays	R4C	2nd
		Bira	R2B	3rd
28th August	J.C.C. 200 Mile Race, Donington Park	Dobson	R12C	1st
		Whitehead	R10B	3rd
11th September	Phoenix Park, Dublin, Ireland	Mays	R4C	1st
		Cotton	R1B	3rd
26th September	Masaryk G.P., Brno, Czechoslovakia	Martin	R3A	2nd
1938				
23rd April	Cork G.P., Carrigrohane, Cork, Ireland	Bira	R12C	1st
		Dobson	R7B	2nd
12th June	G.P. De Picardy, Peronne, France	Mays	R4D	1st
9th July	Nuffield Trophy, Donington Park	Bira	R12C	1st
		Dobson	R7B	3rd
21st August	Prix De Berne, Bremgarten, Switzerland	Wakefield	R14B	3rd
27th August	J.C.C. 200 Mile Race, Brooklands, Campbell Circuit	Wakefield	R14B	1st
		Howe	R8C	3rd
18th September	Circuit of Modena, Italy	Dobson	R7B	3rd
1939				
14th January	Grosvenor G.P., South Africa	Aitken	R11B	2nd
10th June	Nuffield Trophy, Donington Park	Bira	R12C	1st
		Mays	R4D	2nd
		Whitehead	R10B	3rd
16th July	G.P. d'Albigeois, Albi, France	Bira	R2B	3rd

CHAPTER TWENTY SIX

The E-Type G.P.1 & G.P.2

With the A,B,C and D type E.R.A.'s outdated and uncompetitive by the late thirties, a new car was needed to uphold Britain's honour in the racing world.

Reid Railton, the original E.R.A. chassis designer went to the U.S.A. to work on other projects and the talented Murray Jamieson sadly was killed as a spectator in an accident at Brooklands. Peter Berthon, the remaining engineer, was then a little lost, the others' input in the original project having been so important. Simultaneously, much talk of building a Grand Prix challenger to beat the German Mercedes-Benz and Auto-Union teams was leaked to the press.

I would guess that Humphrey Cook was getting cold feet about further investment, having spent £90,000 of his own money so far on E.R.A.'s. British industry was also showing no interest in supporting the idea, preferring to prepare itself for the looming war.

30th July 1938. Raymond Mays testing the unpainted G.P.1 at Donington Park.

When the first E-Type E.R.A. chassis number G.P.1. appeared eventually in 1939, it was not a Grand Prix car but was fitted with a 1,500cc supercharged engine of similar design to that used before. The car was lower than previous E.R.A.'s and clothed in a Mercedes-Benz style body. It looked the part but against its opposition from Europe G.P.1. was a disaster; it was too little, too late. It was no match for the Alfa Romeo 158, Maserati 4CL of Italy or the Mercedes-Benz W165 of Germany.

G.P.1.'s failure brought about the separation of Raymond Mays and Humphrey Cook following the car's first event at Brooklands. Mays left the team with R4D and Cook set up shop at Donington Park with G.P.1. The car appeared at four events, two each in England and France. Three times the car did not start its race due to overheating or engine problems and in its only race at Albi, France, Arthur Dobson crashed. A sad end to the E.R.A. story pre-war.

G.P.1. raced after the war alongside a second E-Type G.P.2.

Post-war photograph of Peter Walker in G.P.1.

The cars faired no better post-war than they did pre-war though the cars were driven by some of Britain's best drivers – Peter Whitehead, Peter Walker, Reg Parnell, H.L. Brooke plus the new E.R.A. owner, Leslie Johnson.

Retirements seemed to be the norm from both cars.

The histories of both G.P.1 and G.P.2. really come to an end in 1950 with G.P.1. being burnt out in an accident though a spare chassis for G.P.3. has been used to rebuild G.P.1.. G.P.2. was retired in 1950 and has now been totally rebuilt. Both cars are owned by Gordon J. Chapman.

CHAPTER TWENTY SEVEN

The G-Type

Humphrey Cook moved E.R.A. to Dunstable in 1946, the town where the firm still operates. In 1947 Leslie Johnson, an amateur racing driver, took over the firm and the E-Type project. He had plans to build his own Formula One car but in the meantime an F-Type Formula Three car got no further than the drawing board. The G-Type was to be a Formula Two car using a Bristol 2 litre 6 cylinder engine as used in the successful Cooper-Bristol. During 1952 and 1953 Grand Prix racing was run to Formula Two regulations.

The car showed promise in the hands of a young Stirling Moss during the 1952 season.

1952 Stirling Moss in the 'G-type'

At the end of 1952 E.R.A. concentrated on their 2½ litre Grand Prix project and the G-Type was sold to the Bristol Aircraft Co. to become the basis for their successful attack on the Le Mans 24hr race with their Type 450. In 1954 the Bristol 450 achieved 1st, 2nd and 3rd in class, 7th, 8th and 9th overall at Le Mans.

In 1953 Leslie Johnson suffered a heart attack and E.R.A. was sold to the Zenith Carburettor Co. who in turn were bought by the Solex Carburettor Co. The 2½ litre Grand Prix car was then forgotten.

1954 The Bristol 450 based on the G-type E.R.A.

CHAPTER TWENTY EIGHT

The M-Type

Thirty-five years after E.R.A.'s last car project, the firm returned with a new car based on the Austin Rover Mini. It is called the M-Type or E.R.A. Mini Turbo.

On the 2nd September 1959 B.M.C. launched the Mini, created by the great designer, Sir Alec Issigonis. Engineering Research Applications, with their expertise in automobile engineering, have designed and built their own version of this timeless classic.

The car incorporates E.R.A.'s thinking on engine/turbo management, suspension and brakes, plus subtle bodywork changes for high speed stability.

The 'A' series 1275c.c. engine has been fitted with a Garrett turbocharger developing 94b.h.p., at 6,130 r.p.m. at maximum boost pressure of 8 p.s.i., with a top speed of 115m.p.h.

1990 Silverstone.
M-Type Mini with A.J.M.1
in the background.

The car is hand built to a very high standard at E.R.A.'s Dunstable factory.
The E.R.A. story continues.

*1990 E.R.A. Minis await
export to Japan.*

Bibliography

The Story of E.R.A.,
John Lloyd,
Motor Racing Publications 1949.

The History of English Racing Automobiles Limited,
David Weguelin,
White Mouse Editions 1980.

The Racing Fitfteen-Hundreds,
David Venables,
Transport Bookman Publications 1984.

The History of Brooklands Motor Course,
William Boddy,
Grenville Publishing Co Ltd 1957.

Bits and Pieces,
Prince Birabongse of Thailand,
Foulis 1942.

Mostly Motor Racing,
Rivars Fletcher,
Haynes 1986.

Directory of Historic Racing Cars,
Denis Jenkinson,
Aston 1987.

Automobile Quarterly Vol. 13, No. 3,
Automoblile Quarterly 1975.

Split Seconds,
Raymond Mays,
Foulis 1951.

At Speed,
Raymond Mays,
Hodder and Stoughton 1952.

Magazines
Classic and Sportscar
Old Motor
Motor
Autocar
Motor Sport
Classic Cars